IMAGES
of Aviation

THE ROYAL
FLYING CORPS

One of the few official aerial combat photographs taken in the First World War. The aircraft in the distance is a Rumpler two-seat, whilst the pursuing aircraft is an Armstrong Whitworth FK.8.

IMAGES
of Aviation

THE ROYAL
FLYING CORPS

Compiled by
Terry C. Treadwell & Alan C. Wood

TEMPUS

First published 2000
Copyright © Terry C. Treadwell & Alan C. Wood, 2000

Tempus Publishing Limited
The Mill, Brimscombe Port,
Stroud, Gloucestershire, GL5 2QG

ISBN 0 7524 1733 9

Typesetting and origination by
Tempus Publishing Limited
Printed in Great Britain by
Midway Clark Printing, Wiltshire

Contents

Sopwith 7F1 Snipe making a low pass over Stonehenge Airfield.

Introduction

British Military aviation stems from the first usage of observation balloons by the Royal Engineers (RE) who had five such balloons at Woolwich Arsenal in 1879.

The Army interest in balloons had commenced in 1863 when a Mr Henry Coxwell was commissioned by the Army to make a series of ascents at Aldershot. One ascent was made by two officers from the Royal Engineers who made a favourable report.

In 1884 the Bechuanaland Expedition included a detachment of three balloons with a complement of sixteen personnel under the command of a Major Elsdale RE. Other campaigns saw the use of balloons.

Meeting with success, the Balloon Section was enlarged and moved to the open spaces of Aldershot in 1881. During 1890 a Balloon Section was officially established as a unit of the Royal Engineers. During the winter of 1905-1906 the Balloon Section RE moved to Farnborough, Hampshire, where the RE Balloon Factory was firmly established.

On 1 April 1911 the aviation element of the Royal Engineers was expanded to battalion strength with Headquarters at South Farnborough, No.1 (Airship) Company, also at Farnborough, and No.2 (Aeroplane) Company at Larkhill, near Stonehenge, Salisbury Plain, Wiltshire. This was the first British military unit equipped with heavier-than-air craft. Commander of the Royal Engineers Air Battalion was Major Sir Alexander Bannerman, while Captain E.M. Maitland commanded the Airship Company and Captain J.D.B. Fulton the Aeroplane Company.

On 13 April 1912 the Royal Flying Corps (RFC) was constituted by Royal Warrant. The British Governmental intention was that such a Corps could serve both Army and Navy requirements: an obvious cost-cutting plan. Accordingly, the original Royal Flying Corps consisted of a Military Wing, Naval Wing and a Central Flying School for training all pilots. One month later, on 13 May, the RFC absorbed the Royal Engineers Air Battalion and the Government voted to allocate £308,000 to the new Corps.

This unwieldy state of affairs continued until 23 June 1914 when the Admiralty insisted that the Naval Wing become a service in its own right. The Royal Naval Air Service then came into being on 1 July leaving the Royal Flying Corps comprising of the Military Wing and Central Flying School at Upavon, Wiltshire.

When the Royal Flying Corps was created, in April 1912, the Aeroplane Company of the Air Battalion, Royal Engineers became No.3 Squadron RFC. No.2 Squadron RFC was formed by pilots from the Air Battalion Depot at Farnborough. No.1 Squadron RFC was formed from No.1 Airship Company, Air Battalion, Royal Engineers and remained as the RFC Airship Detachment until 1 May 1914. On the same day a cadre No.1 Squadron was formed at Brooklands with heavier-than-air craft. It is open to question whether No.1 Squadron was the first RFC Squadron: it depends on what constitutes a squadron, heavier or lighter-than-air craft.

All Airships became the responsibility of the Royal Navy on 1 January 1914 and, by the end of 1913, the RFC had transferred all its airships to the Navy. Four more squadrons – Nos 4, 5, 6 and 7 – were created before the outbreak of war in August 1914 making RFC strength seven squadrons in total.

On the outbreak of the First World War, Nos 2, 3, 4 and 5 Squadrons moved to France making the strength of the RFC there sixty-three aeroplanes, ninety-five vehicles, 105 officers and 755 other ranks commanded by Brigadier General Sir David Henderson.

In November 1914 two Wings of two squadrons each were formed, 1st Wing to serve with the First Army and 2nd Wing with the Second Army. The Royal Flying Corps was initially at war in small numbers but, by the end of hostilities, it had become the largest air force in the world.

Henri Farman of No.4 Squadron RFC dipping its nose in salute to General Sir Horace Smith-Dorrien (Reviewing Officer) at the first 'air review' for RFC.

Lieutenant Gwilym Hugh Lewis, RFC, on flying instruction.

Breguet biplane being towed back to its hangar after landing with engine trouble while on trials at Farnborough.

Senior officers of the Royal Flying Corps at Netheravon in 1913. On the right Major F. Sykes can be seen talking to Major-General Sefton Brancker.

BE.2a No.468 outside the sheds of the CFS at Upavon in 1913.

A, B & C Flights of the CFS at Upavon in 1914.

BE.2a aircraft at airfield on Salisbury Plain.

Bleriot XI on Salisbury Plain.

Maurice Farman No.22 at the 1912 military trials.

Bristol Coanda monoplane No.106 at the 1912 military trials. The number on the tail possibly refers to the trials number.

Bristol Coanda monoplane No.105 at the 1912 military trials.

Coventry Ordnance Works Biplane No.11 at military trials.

Breguet biplane B.3 at the Army trials. It is seen here while being prepared for the trials.

S.E.1 biplane being readied for trials. This aircraft had been designed and built at Farnborough.

Bristol Tractor Biplane preparing for take-off during trials.

Bleriot Monoplane at the Army Trials.

The first military trials for the RFC in August 1912. Monsieur Prevost landing his 100hp Gnome Deperdussin during the 'ploughed field' section of the trials. He eventually took second prize, the first going to Cody's Cathedral aircraft.

S.F. Cody demonstrating his Cathedral aircraft at Hendon.

Lieutenant Carmichael of No.3 Squadron, RFC, about to take off in a Henri Farman at Army trials at Abbey Field, Colchester, in June 1913.

Henri Farman flight, No.3 Squadron, RFC, being inspected by HM King George V at Farnborough in May 1913. On the left, facing the camera, is General Sir John French with HM Queen Mary. King George V can be seen on the right.

One

Genesis: Beginnings of an Air Corps.

One of the leading supporters of an air force in the early 1900s was a Royal Field Artillery officer, Captain Bertram Dickson. In a memorandum to a sub-committee of the Imperial Defence Committee, Dickson emphasized Britain's need for an air force as 'The fight for supremacy of the air in future wars will be of the first and greatest importance.'

Dickson was no stranger to upsetting the status quo: he had learned to fly at his own expense at Chalons-sur-Marne in 1909 and had been reprimanded the following year for flying over British Army annual manoeuvres in a Bristol aircraft and 'Unnecessarily frightening the cavalry's horses'.

The Imperial Defence Committee had been tasked with creating efficient army and naval air services and evaluating the need for aerial navigation for their usage.

In Germany – the apparent war opponent – development of lighter-than-air rigid airships was progressing rapidly, with nearly all such aircraft capable of carrying out reconnaissance and bombing flights over the North Sea and English Channel. The German aircraft could carry a small-bomb load, while the British aircraft had virtually nothing in comparison.

On 28 February 1911 the British War Office created, by Special Order, an Air Detachment from personnel of the British Army's Corps of Royal Engineers. On 1 April 1911 the Air Detachment was increased to become an Air Battalion.

The far sighted Imperial Defence Sub Committee decided that a mere Air Battalion was insufficient for military needs and decreed it be replaced with a 'Flying Corps' separate from the Army. The army descriptive term 'Corps' had to be used as no one then knew what else to call the new Service.

Accordingly, on 13 April 1912, the Royal Flying Corps (RFC) came into being and on 13 May 1912, it absorbed the Royal Engineers Air Battalion.

To administer the Royal Flying Corps, a new organization – the Air Ministry – was formed and a Royal Aircraft Factory created at Farnborough, Hampshire, to carry out all research on aeronautics.

The original Royal Flying Corps was formed of three Wings: a Military Wing based at Larkhill, Wiltshire, a Naval Wing at Eastchurch, Kent, and a Central Flying School (CFS) at Upavon, Wiltshire. The Naval Wing maintained from the beginning an independent autonomy which eventually resulted in the formation of the Royal Naval Air Service on 23 June 1914, and into being on 1 July 1914.

By the beginning of 1912 the Royal Flying Corps had eighteen aircraft on charge – fourteen of which were monoplanes. Owing to aircraft accidents, the RFC was prohibited from flying its monoplanes which were deemed to be unsafe. The Corps was now left with four biplanes of No.3 Squadron – which lays claim to being the first true aeroplane squadron in British military history.

In time, with the further formation of squadrons, the fledgling Corps slowly built up its aircraft strength. BE (British Experimental) 2s, Maurice Farmans, Breguets and Avros were obtained and built up into a pool of aircraft. This progress was reflected when 4 Squadron was able to detach two complete Flights – consisting of eight aircraft – to the new Royal Naval Air Service.

In June 1914 the entire might of the RFC Military Wing was assembled at a 'Concentration Camp' (A Boer War term which had evil connections in the Second World War) at Netheravon, on Salisbury Plain. Nos 2, 3, 4, 5 and 6 Squadrons were present, while No.1 Squadron was converted from airships and No.7 Squadron was formed at Farnborough. The assembled 700 officers and men of the RFC were put through a month's intensive programme. They finished in time for the obvious looming war with Germany.

On 4 August 1914 Britain was at war with Germany. The RNAS assumed a Home Defence role – with the RFC ordered to support the British Army in France. 'An aerial cavalry reconnaissance unit' as one senior officer described their role.

However, before the First World War ended, the RFC and later RAF fought in East Africa, Italy, Mesopotamia, Palestine and Russia. Some cavalry unit!

Lieutenant Gwilym Hugh Lewis (on the left) and his brother, Lieutenant Edmund L. Lewis standing in front of a Caudron trainer.

Eight Henri Farman biplanes and four BE.2as of No.5 Squadron, RFC, lined up on the airfield at Farnborough in 1914.

FE.2b caught in the sights of a Hythe gun camera.

THE OFFICERS, ROYAL FLYING CORPS (M.W.)

CONCENTRATION CAMP, NETHERAVON, 1914

Lieut. Mansergh (att.) Lieut. Carpenter (att.) Lieut. Shekleton Lieut. Atkinson Lieut. Hartree Lieut. Moore (att.) Lieut. Hoskins Lieut. Waterfall (att.) Lieut. Lywood (att.) Lieut. Hordern

Lieut. Harvey-Kelly Lieut. Freeman Lieut. McNeece Lieut. Glanville Lieut. Noel Lieut. Wadham Lieut. Porter Lieut. Playfair Lieut. Hubbard Lieut. Lewis Lieut. Morgan Lieut. Small

Lieut. Penn-Gaskell Lieut. Dawes Lieut. Martyn Lieut. Vaughan Lieut. Birch Lieut. Read Lieut. Adams Lieut. Borton Lieut. Corballis Lieut. Mapplebeck

Lieut. Smith (att.) Lieut. Christie Lieut. Stodart Lieut. Rodwell Lieut. James Lieut. Spence Lieut. Mansfield Lieut. Humphreys Lieut. Gould Lieut. Mitchell Lieut. Cogan Lieut. Small (R. G. D.) Lieut. Allen Lieut. & Qr. Mr. Pry

Capt. Holt Capt. Shephard Capt. Grey Capt. Stopford Capt. Bete Capt. Todd Capt. Waldron Lieut. Hynes Lieut. Mills Lieut. Joubert de la Ferté Lieut. Fuller

Capt. Beatty Capt. Dawes Major Hon. C. Brabazon Major Musgrave Major Raleigh Major Higgins Lieut.-Col. Sykes Lieut. & Adjt. Barrington-Kennett Capt. Conner Capt. Cholmondeley Capt. Herbert Capt. Charlton Capt. Carmichael

The officers of the Royal Flying Corps (MW) at the Concentration Camp at Netheravon in 1914. They are all named.

Second-Lieutenant J. Sellers, of C Flight, No.3 Squadron, RFC, about to start the engine of his Sopwith 1F Camel.

RFC HQ Flight, Netheravon Concentration Camp. Seated in the centre is Officer Commanding Major F. Sykes.

Reconnaissance crew with their cameras aboard an Armstrong Whitworth FK.3, No.B9554, setting the cameras prior to leaving on a photo-reconnaissance flight.

Henri Farman trainer about to take off on an instruction flight.

Wreckage of a DH.2 with the body of the RFC pilot lying alongside.

Bristol Scout C of No.5 Squadron, RFC, early in 1914. Attached to the engine cowling can be seen a Lee-Enfield .303 rifle without a stock, fitted at an angle so as to miss the propeller when fired. Just below the rifle can be seen a Mauser pistol in a holster and rag-tailed hand grenades.

Caudron G.III trainer in flight.

General Sir David Henderson presenting Sergeant Dean with the Military Medal for bravery in France.

Royal Aircraft Factory FE.2a of the RFC, on a training flight over England.

Lieutenant Winter (holding the camera) and Captain Mackay in a Maurice Farman. They are about to go on a photo-reconnaissance patrol.

RFC mechanics fully 'booted and spurred' just about to be posted to France. Note that all have been issued with sidearms (revolvers).

Royal Flying Corps lorry park at Netheravon in 1914.

No.2 Squadron, RFC, roll call at Montrose, Scotland, in 1914. The lorries were mainly Leylands.

The crew of an FB.5 believed to be of No.11 Squadron, RFC, while demonstrating the components of a Lewis machine gun.

Henri Farman No.284, of No.5 Squadron, RFC, being flown by Lieutenant G.I. Carmichael.

Instructor and pupil about to take off on a dual flight in a Maurice Farman Shorthorn at Upavon.

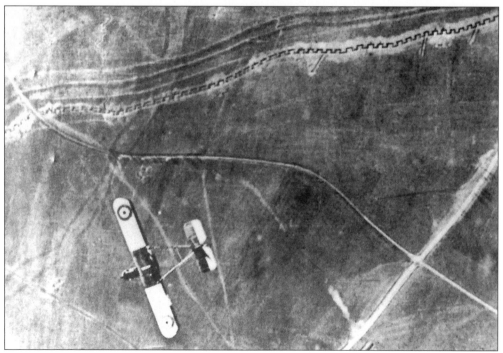

FE.2b on a reconnaissance flight over the front lines.

FB.26A Vampire II with a Bentley B.R.2 rotary engine and armed with twin machine guns.

Nieuport 27 Scout No.B6768, of No.1 Squadron, RFC. The aircraft in the background are SE.5s.

Senior members of No.5 Squadron, RFC, at lunch during the retreat from Mons in 1914. From left to right: Rabagnati, Wilson, Conner, Major Higgins.

Members of No.5 Squadron, RFC, grabbing a bite to eat during the retreat from Mons.

Two

War:
The First Air War Begins.

At the outbreak of the First World War the RFC had Nos 2 and 4 Squadrons equipped with B.E.2 biplanes; No.3 Squadron with Bleriots and Henri Farmans and No.5 Squadron with Henri Farmans, Avro 504s and B.E. 8s.

No.6 Squadron's personnel and airplanes had been dispersed among the other squadrons to bring them up to strength. Later the squadron acquired R.E.5s, then B.E.s and Bleriots.

On 11 August 1914 the first RFC ground staff embarked at Southampton for France. The RFC's aircraft strength in France was sixty-three, with a mobilized uniformed strength of 860 officers and men, under the command of Brigadier General Sir David Henderson, Argyll & Sutherland Highlanders.

Lieutenant-Colonel H.M. Trenchard – one of the first instructors at CFS Upavon – was appointed to command all that was left of the RFC in Britain. Later, from 19 August 1915, he would command the RFC in France and become known as the 'Father of the Royal Air Force'.

Opposing the RFC in France would be the Imperial German Air Service with approximately 1000 aircraft – with the advantage of mainly fighting over their own front lines.

The first RFC casualties of the First World War were Lt R.R.Skene and Air Mechanic Barlow – killed in their Bleriot aircraft flying to Dover en route for France.

On 13 August 1914 the first RFC Squadrons began to fly to France; the first aircraft to land at Amiens at 8.20 a.m. was a B.E.2a, No.347 of No.3 Squadron, flown by Lt H.D. Harvey Kelley. On 19 August 1914 the RFC lost its first aircraft in action, when an Avro 504 of No.5 Squadron, flown by Lt V. Waterfall, was shot down by ground fire in Belgium.

By early March 1915, the RFCs Order of Battle showed seven squadrons in the field in France with a total complement of eighty-five aircraft of twelve different types. Six months later there were twelve squadrons totalling 161 aircraft with some fourteen different types. No.11 Squadron RFC was completely equipped with Vickers F.B.5s – the first fighter squadron to be so equipped with a single purpose aircraft.

The first RFC Victoria Cross (VC) was awarded posthumously to Lt W.B. Rhodes

Moorhouse of 2 Squadron flying a B.E.2 on a low level bombing raid on Courtrai railway station on 26 April 1915. One year later, most RFC squadrons were single purpose squadrons, each equipped with but one type of aircraft.

On 1 July 1916 the Battle of the Somme began. The RFC strength was some 421 aircraft in twenty-seven squadrons at home and in France.

The Squadrons and aircraft types in France were as follows:

No.1 Squadron. Nieuport 12 & Morane Parasol.
No.3 Squadron. Morane Parasol.
No.60 Squadron Morane Parasol.
No.11 Squadron. F.E.2b.
No.18 Squadron F.E.2b.
No.22 Squadron F.E.2b.
No.23 Squadron F.E.2b.
No.25 Squadron F.E.2b.
No.15 Squadron. Bristol Scout.
No.20 Squadron. F.E.2d
No.24 Squadron. D.H.2
No.27 Squadron. Martinsyde G.100
No.29 Squadron. D.H.2 / 32 Squadron D.H.2
No.70 Squadron. Sopwith 1½Strutter.

The ferocious land battle sucked in seven more RFC squadrons and seven RNAS squadrons in a struggle of attrition. By the end of November 1916, the RFC and RNAS had established air superiority over the opposing German Air Service.

Shortly to emerge were the Bristol Fighter, the SE.5, Sopwith Pup and Triplane. Later came the superb Sopwith F.1 Camel whose pilots shot down more enemy aircraft than did any other single British type used in the First World War.

By April 1917 the strength of the RFC at the Battle of Arras had increased to over 900 aircraft, organized into five Brigades of ten Squadrons. The R.E.8 biplane with a 150hp engine was coming on service and proved a stable flying and gun platform.

April 1917, however, proved to be the lowest point of the RFCs fortunes: a third of its aircrews fell to the German Air Service aircraft, with their Albatros D.111 outclassing the RFC's aircraft.

The Third Battle of Ypres – better known as Passchendaele – (July-November 1917) saw the RFC regain its spurs in air combat flying the SE.5, the Spad, the Sopwith Pup and Camel, Nieuport Scout and D.H.5.

Graham White GW
XV Trainer,
No.8305, being
fuelled for an
instruction lesson.

Lieutenant E. Henty
of No.32 Squadron,
RFC, climbing
aboard his DH.2.

Lieutenant E. Henty of No.32 Squadron, RFC, adjusting some of his controls on his DH.2.

Lieutenant Augustus 'Nigger' Horn's SE5A, of 85 Squadron, RFC, after an horrendous crash from which he walked away unscathed. Horn was an American who had been trained in Canada and then posted to the RFC.

Sopwith F1 Camel '6' of No.28 Squadron, RFC, having nosed over on landing.

Nieuport 17, No.B1690, RFC, after a landing mishap. Note the unusual variance in the sizes of the cockade on the upper wing.

DH.1A heading over the lines on patrol in the early mist of the morning.

Captain Hermann W. von Poellnitz in the cockpit of his DH.2 at Vert Galland Ferme in 1916.

A female member
of the RFC Motor
Transport section
awaiting in
London, by the
looks of the car, a
senior officer.

Two RFC pilots
are 'caught' in a
London street by
flag-sellers
on St. Patrick's
Day – 17 March
1916.

DH.2s of No.29 Squadron, RFC, at Abeele, France – 1916.

Air crews of No.16 Squadron, RFC, at Beaupre Farm, La Gorgue, in June 1916. From left to right: Least, Owles, Buck, Howell, Minot, Budgen, Davidson, Major Powell (CO), Diamond, Shaw, Ellis, Nesbitt, Pentland, Waller, Trascott, Waddington, Welsh.

A remarkable air-to-air photograph of an allied aircraft with smoke pouring from the engine, while the German attacker watches from above.

The funeral of 2nd Lt Ivan Carryer, RFC. Carryer was killed when his aircraft hit a shed and burst into flames.

Sopwith 1½Strutter of 70 Squadron, RFC, at Brooklands in 1916.

Major Murlis Green, DSO, MC, OC of No.44 Squadron, taking off in his modified Sopwith 1F1 Camel from Hainault Farm. Note the two top-wing-mounted Lewis machine guns and the two pennants streaming from the outer wing struts.

BE.2c with a fixed camera.

Sage Type 2 fighter developed for the RFC. This aircraft first flew on 10 August 1916, but was wrecked one month later. It was never considered a serious proposition as a fighter.

Morane 'P' fighter No.B1615 of No.3 Squadron, RFC, preparing for a mission.

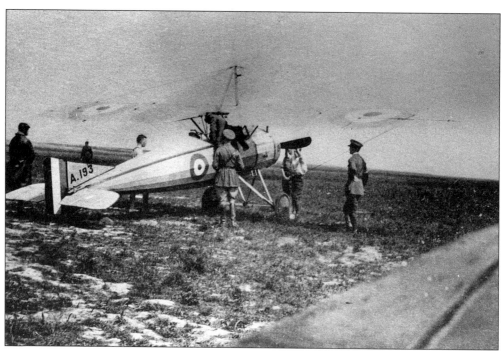
Morane 'P', No.A193, of No.3 Squadron, RFC, with General Ashmore climbing into the cockpit.

Morane Parasols of No.3 Squadron, RFC, at La Houssoye, France, in September 1916.

Major R.G. Blomfield, RFC, OC No.20 Reserve Squadron, Wye, on one of their weekly route marches through Wye village, Kent, in August 1916.

Pilots of No.56 Squadron, RFC. Captain Albert Ball, VC, is seated with his hands in his pockets, second from the right.

Officers of No.32 Squadron, RFC, at Vert Galand Ferme. From left to right: 2nd Lt Bonnel, Lt Inman, Lt J.J.G. Maremontemboult, Captain F.H. Coleman, Captain J.M. Robb, Lt A.P. Aizlewood, Lt C.N. Jones, Lt R.H. Wallace, Lt Nicholas, Lt E. Henty, Lt Martin, Major T.A.E. Cairnes, Lt G. Allen, Lt C.L. Bath, Lt H.W. Poellnitz, Lt O.V. Thomas, Lt G.H. Lewis, Lt P.B.G. Hunt.

BE.2e carrying out a reconnaissance flight over the trenches in France.

BE.2c crash at Yatesbury, Wiltshire. The frailty of these aircraft can be seen in this photograph by the way the tail section has snapped clean in half.

Salvage party having recovered the crashed BE.2c aircraft and loaded it onto the back of a Leyland lorry, prepare to take it back to a salvage depot.

Bleriot Type Parasol at Redcar in 1916 taking off on a flight trial.

FE.2b on its way
across the lines
for a daylight
reconnaissance
mission.

A low-level reconnaissance flight over the trenches.

The pilot's cockpit of the FE.2b. The two mountings in front were for the hand-operated Lewis machine guns.

Lieutenant H.W. Poellnitz of No.32 Squadron, RFC, taking off from Vert Galand Ferme airfield, France, in July 1916.

Officers from No.84 Squadron, RFC, with a captured Fokker D.VII.

DH.2s of No.32 Squadron, RFC, at Vert Galand, France in 1916. At the right, the centre figure is Major T.A.E. Cairnes, the Commanding Officer.

Lieutenant L.P. Aizelwood, MC, seated in a DH.2 Scout of No.32 Squadron, RFC.

Ground crew and pilots of No.15 Squadron, RFC, with one of the aircraft, an RE.8, No.A4704.

Members of the ground crew of No.43 Squadron, RFC.

Lieutenant Jenkinson, RFC, looking elated climbing out of his Sopwith 1F1 Camel after a sortie.

RE.8 climbing away.

Flight Commander H. McClelland in front of his night-flying BE.2c.

Captain D.R. McLaren of No.46 Squadron, RFC, standing holding the propeller of his Sopwith Pup. Although never recognized as a top ace, he accounted for fifty-four enemy aircraft.

RE.8 of A Flight, No.59 Squadron about to go over the front.

An RE.8 of No.3 Squadron, AFC, about to start their engine on Savy airfield, France.

Bombing up an RE.8 of No.3 Squadron, AFC.

Vickers FB.5 'Gunbus' No.5677, RFC, being prepared for flight.

'I think we are somewhere... here'. Pilots of No.32 Squadron studying a map prior to one of their DH.2 aircraft going a reconnaissance flight. The pilot can be seen sitting calmly in his seat, while the others possibly discuss his fate. From left to right: Wilson, Thomas, -?-, Bonnalie, Martin, Coleman, Lewis, Allen, Sergeant Dobson. Note the very large webbing seatbelt hanging over the side of the cockpit.

DH.2 No.5994 of 29 Squadron, RFC, surrounded by German soldiers after being shot down by Hauptmann Zander of Jasta 1. on 25 August 1916. The pilot, 2nd Lt E.K. Turner, RFC, was captured and made Prisoner of War.

An RFC firing party gives the final volley over the grave of Captain Gilbert William Mapplebeck, DSO, at Streatham Cemetry, London. Mapplebeck died while testing a Moranne monoplane.

SE5A, No.B8388 'F' after a bad landing.

SE5A 'O' of 84
Squadron, RFC, being
recovered after
crashing.

A BE.2e precariously
balanced in the top of a
tree after a 'slight'
misjudgment on
approaching the
airfield. The pilot is still
in the cockpit trying to
figure out how to get
down the tree, while
rescuers are climbing
the tree trying to figure
out how to get the
aircraft down.

Bristol F2b fighter No.B1180 with its nose buried in the ground after the undercarriage collapsed on landing.

A rather relieved pilot stands at the tail of his Vickers FB.9, No.7834 after paying an unscheduled visit to HQ.

Landing mishap of a Nieuport 17.

No.12 Squadron, RFC, workshop lorry at Netheravon in 1915.

RE.8, A4267, '7', after landing from a sortie. It was part of No.52 Squadron, RFC, which operated as an army-cooperation squadron on the Western Front.

Three

Combat:
The Aircrews and
Aircraft.

Necessity is the mother of invention and, as far as war is concerned, there was never a truer statement. War also brings out the best and the worst in people and turns ordinary men and women into heroes. This was never more so than in the First World War, whether it was on the ground, on the sea, or in the air.

The Royal Flying Corps started life with nothing but a few flimsy aircraft and some balloons. When war was declared, the fighter aircraft itself had been developed to a degree but the art of fighting in the air was an unknown quantity. It was those who were able to grasp and understand the rudiments of this new form of warfare that stood the greatest chance of survival. Some of these men were to become the Aces. At the beginning of the First World War, the Royal Flying Corps in France consisted of sixty-three aircraft and 860 officers and men.

The first recorded incident involving a British and German aircraft, was on 25 August 1914 when Lieutenant Harvey-Kelly, RFC, and two other members of No.2 Squadron intercepted an unarmed German Rumpler observation aircraft while on a reconnaissance flight. The three British aircraft, also unarmed, dived repeatedly at the Rumpler and flew circles around it until the pilot was forced to land in a field. Upon doing so, the German pilot and his observer ran away, while Lieutenant Harvey-Kelly landed his aircraft alongside and set fire to the German aircraft. This was the first German aircraft to be brought down in the war, albeit without firing a shot.

As war progressed the number of losses increased daily, taking its toll on the general morale of those back in Britain. A new word 'Ace' came into being. French journalists created the word for the French pilot Roland-Garros, after he had shot down his third enemy aircraft. It was picked up by an unknown American war correspondent, who stated that a pilot who shot down five enemy aircraft was an Ace. The British did not like the word and would not use it. The Germans, on the other hand, revelled in the term and saw the use of it in propaganda. However, they set out the requirement that ten victories were needed for a pilot to become a *Kanone* (Ace).

One of the first Allied 'aces' was a shy young man, Captain Albert Ball, VC, DSO, MC. He flew a variety of aircraft in his short but illustrious career, among these were the Nieuport Scout, RE.8 and SE5. He received his wings in January 1916 and died on 7 May 1917. During that time he had risen to the rank of captain and had shot down forty-four German aircraft. He was just twenty years old.

There were over 200 'Aces' in the RFC during the First World War, if one were to use the 'five kills' requirement as a measure. Only a relatively small number of these pilots scored over twenty. Among them were those who became household names, like Major Lanoe George Hawker, VC, DSO, who, although only scoring 'seven kills', was regarded as Britain's first 'Ace'. He was to die under the guns of Manfred von Richthofen – The Red Baron. Then there was William Avery Bishop, VC, DSO, MC, a Canadian who joined the RFC in July 1915 as an observer but soon progressed to become a pilot. His tally at the end of the war was the highest in the RFC with seventy-two victories. Major George William Barker, VC, DSO, MC, counted fifty victories, flying Sopwith Camels and Snipes while Captain Anthony Frederick Weatherby Beauchamp-Proctor, VC, DSO, MC, had a total of fifty-four victories flying SE5s. Major James Thomas Byford McCudden, VC, DSO, MC, scored fifty-seven kills flying a DH.2. One of the most famous of all the RFC's pilots was Major Edward 'Micky' Mannock, VC, DSO, MC, who in just eighteen months destroyed sixty-one enemy aircraft, before he himself was brought down and killed by ground fire.

There were others who never became household names but contributed just as much and in some case even more. Captain Alfred Clayburn Atkey, MC, claimed thirty-eight victories flying DH.4s and Bristol F2Bs while Lieutenant Leonard Monteagle Barlow, MC, claimed twenty flying an SE5. Captain John Douglas Bell, MC, a South African who joined the RFC in June 1916 and was shot down less than a year later, accounted for twenty enemy aircraft in that short period of time. Major Geoffrey Hilton Bowman, DSO, DFC, shot down thirty-two enemy aircraft, while Captain William Gordon Claxton, DSO, DFC, a Canadian, shot down thirty-seven. Captain Philip Fletcher Fullard, DSO, MC, was flying the Nieuport and his tally reached forty in just six months. Major Tom Falcon Hazell, DSO, DFC, from Ireland, flew Nieuports and SE5s and accounted for forty-three enemy aircraft, while the Canadian Major Donald Roderick Maclaren, DSO, DFC, MC, accounted for fifty-four enemy aircraft and balloons in one year. One member of the Commonwealth who joined the RFC at the outbreak of war, was 2nd-Lieutenant Indra Lal Roy from Calcutta, India. He was at school in England when the war broke out and immediately joined up. On graduating as a pilot, he joined No.40 Squadron and, in the month of July 1918, accounted for ten German aircraft before he himself was shot down and killed. He was the first Indian 'Ace'.

What is very apparent, is that a number of the pilots came from Commonwealth countries and it was this bond that gave Britain the necessary resolve to win the war.

We feel it is also necessary at this stage to understand the types of aircraft that these pilots were flying. Flimsy and crude are two words that readily spring to mind. Couple these with the horrendous conditions that the crews had to operate and live under, and one gets some indication of the sturdiness of the aircraft and the kind of men who flew and maintained them.

The Sopwith Camel was one of the most respected, but most unforgiving aircraft, in the RFC's pool. Tough, fast and reliable, it was a pilot's aircraft and could be devastating in the right hands. The FE.2b on the other hand, although looking as if a puff of wind would destroy it, was one of the most durable and respected of aircraft and more than capable of holding its own in a fight. The SE5A was the aircraft most feared by the Germans because of its agility, speed and fire power. Between them, the SE5A, the FE.2b, the French-built Nieuport and the Sopwith Camel accounted for the majority of the German losses.

Here is a list of aircraft flown by the Royal Flying Corps during the First World War:

Sopwith Camel
Sopwith Dolphin.
Sopwith two-seater.
Sopwith Pup.
Sopwith Snipe.
Sopwith 1½ Strutter.
Sopwith Triplane.
SPAD VII & XIII.
SE5 and 5A.
RE.8.
BE.2.
FE.2b.
FE.2d.
FE.8.
Nieuport 17.
Nieuport Scout.
Bristol Scout.
Bristol F2b.
Bristol MIC.
De Havilland (DH) 2.
De Havilland (DH) 4.
De Havilland (DH) 5.
De Havilland (DH) 9.
Vickers FB.5.
Morane Saulnier.
Morane Parasols.

Sopwith 1F1 Camel No.B3823 of No.70 Squadron, being recovered by a German ground crew after it had been shot down by Leutnant Mohnicke of Jasta 11. The pilot of the Sopwith Camel was Lieutenant R.C. Hume who was captured and made Prisoner of War.

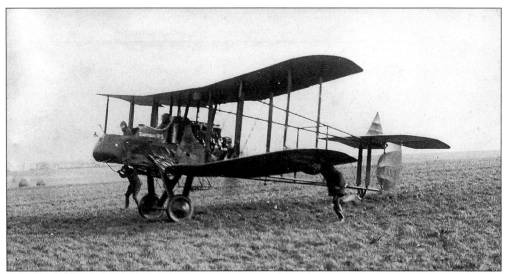

FE.2b 'Zanzibar No.5' of No.100 Squadron, RFC, trundling across the airfield at Aire and about to take off on a test flight.

Sopwith 1F1 Camel about to take off from Petite Synthe to join his partner flying overhead.

Sopwith 1F1 Camels at Petit Synthe, France, about to take off on a mission.

Four gun (one Vickers and three Lewis guns) Bristol F2b Fighter of No.22 Squadron at Agincourt.

RE.8 flying low over the French countryside on a reconnaissance flight.

Sopwith 1F1 Camels of No.73 Squadron, RFC, lined up as a Bristol F2b makes its landing in the background. The aircraft numbers have been scratched out by the censor.

Sopwith 1F1 Camel of No.71 Squadron, RFC, returning to Humieres at dusk, on 6 April 1918, after a mission.

Bristol fighters of No.22 Squadron, RFC, taking off from Serny aerodrome. The Sopwith Camels on the ground belonged to the RNAS.

Bristol Fighter side-slipping away to carry out a low-level reconnaissance patrol.

Bristol F2bs of No.141 Squadron, RFC, at Biggin Hill at the beginning of 1918, preparing for take-off.

Bristol F2bs of B Flight, No.22 Squadron, taking off from Serny airfield, France on an operation, 17 June 1918.

Bristol-built BE2e, No.7216 with a pair of Le Prieur rocket rails mounted on the outer wings.

Bristol-built BE2e No.8407, firing a salvo of Le Prieur rockets from the rails fitted on its outer wings.

Lt George Fraser (on the left) in the observer's seat of a BE2 in the Middle East in 1917. Note the huge canvas seatbelt hanging over the side of the pilot's cockpit.

Lt Scotcher in Sopwith F1 Camel 'Pixie III' of No.122 Squadron, RFC. Note the lucky charm swastika painted on the tail fin.

'Joie de Vivre'. Sopwith 1F Camel, RFC, executing the notorious right-handed turn over the English countryside.

F2b coming in to land over the top three Sopwith 1F1 Camels of No.73 Squadron, RFC, at Humieres.

Pilots from No.54 Squadron, RFC, in 1917.

The bomb dump of No.214 Squadron. Lieutenant Christian Burgener (Canadian) is on the left.

Cockpit of Sopwith F1 Camel, No. B3751.

Captain Wendell W. Rogers, MC, a Canadian of No.1 Squadron, RFC, seated in the cockpit of his Nieuport 27 Scout at Bailleul on 27 December 1917.

Members of No.22 Squadron, RFC, emptying their pockets before going on patrol. From left to right: Lt A.P. Stoyle, Lt I.O. Stead, Lt Weaver, Lt H.H. Beddow, Captain W.F.O. Harvey, Captain J.E. Gundon, Lt G. Thomson, Lt C.W.M. Thompson, Captain G.W. Bulmer. Their Bristol F2B Fighters are being prepared behind them.

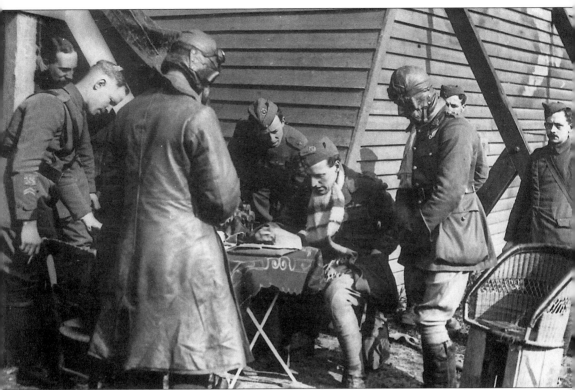

Major V. Stammers (seated) of No.15 Squadron, RFC, studying the patrol reports from the crew of an RE.8.

HM Queen Mary inspecting the RFC Depot at St. Omer on 15 July 1917. At her right elbow is Major-General Hugh Trenchard, who was at the time General Officer Commanding the RFC in France. In the background are a captured Albatros D.III and an AWFK.8 two-seater.

HM Queen Mary with Sir Hugh Trenchard on her left, visiting an RFC squadron at St. Omer, France. The aircraft is an RE.8.

Nieuport 27 Scouts of No.1 Squadron, RFC, lined up on Bailleul airfield on 27 December 1917. The aircraft serial numbers have been scratched out of the original negatives by the censor.

Sopwith 1F1 Camels of No.44 Squadron, RFC, taking off on a sortie.

This crash incident of a DH.6 trainer, lends a whole new meaning to 'Dropping in at the Post Office'!

'Whoops'. American Lieutenant Harrison Brown stands casually beside the wreckage of his BE2 after badly misjudging a landing on a training flight. One wonders if he ever graduated.

Sopwith 1F Camel No.B3840 of No.66 Squadron, RFC, in Italy, being righted after nosing over on landing.

DH.6 No.B2678 after an extremely heavy landing at Chingford.

Rear-view shot of Royal Aircraft Factory FE.2b No.7666 after it had crashed into a garden after suffering engine failure.

FE.2b No.7666 built by Boulton Paul. It is seen here after suffering engine trouble and coming to grief in someone's garden.

SE5As being assembled at the Wolseley Motors Factory.

BE2cs under construction at the Daimler Works.

RE.8s, Nos. F3246 to F3345 on the factory floor at Siddeley-Deasey Motor Car Co. Ltd, Coventry, in early 1918.

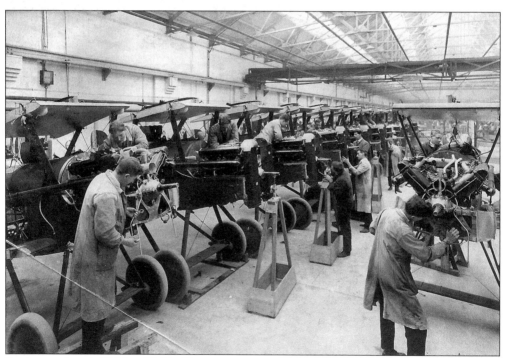

Engineers fitting 200-hp W.4A Viper engines to Wolseley-built SE5 aircraft at Wolseley Motors Ltd in Birmingham.

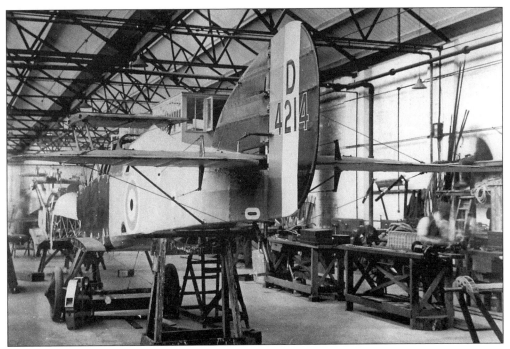

Martinsyde F4 'Buzzard' in workshops under repair.

No.45 Squadron officers mess at Fossalunga, Italy. Clockwise from left to right: G.H. Bush, R.J. Brownell, -?-, J.P. Huins, -?-, Jones, 'Guns' Buck, McLean, Captain Thompson, Renahan – the Mad Irishman, 'Doc' Atlee, M.D.G. Drummond, Jack Cottle. Standing at the back, left to right: Airman Bye (Waiter), Corporal Ames (Waiter), Huband.

Allied pilots – an American, a Canadian, a New Zealander, a South African and an Englishman – examining a map on the fuselage of a Sopwith Pup. A perfect example of the spirit which brought the world together against the enemy.

Royal Aircraft Factory FE.2b No. A5478 on No.100 Squadron (bomber) about to embark on a mission. This obviously posed position of the observer highlights the precarious position he was in during combat.

RFC repair and salvage depot at St. Omer in 1917. From left to right: SE5A, Nieuport Scout and Bristol F2b 'Gold Coast No.11'.

Sopwith 1F1 Camel of No.28 Squadron, RFC, showing extensive flak damage. Second from the left is Lt H.J.L. 'Bert' Hinkler.

Captain George Edward Henry McElroy, MC, DFC, of No.24 Squadron, standing by his SE5A loaded with 4 x 25lb Cooper bombs.

Armourer of No.149 Squadron, RFC, loading bombs on to the bomb rack of an FE.2b at St. Omer, with the pilot and his observer looking on, March 1918.

Major-General F.C. Heath-Caldwell, GOC SE Area, about to present Military Medals to Flight Sergeant Elton and Sergeant Stagg.

Bristol Scout No.B648 of No.4 Squadron, RFC, seen fitted with a stripped-down Lewis machine gun mounted on the outside of the fuselage

Crews and ground crews of No.45 Squadron, RFC, at Istrana, Italy at the beginning of 1918, preparing their Sopwith 1F1 Camels for a mission.

Sergeant Pask, nephew of Field Marshal Sir John French in his SE5A. He was later killed during flight training at Hounslow.

DH.5 No.A9393 being readied for take-off. This aircraft later shed a wing while being looped and crashed, killing the pilot Captain E.G. Hanoln at Sedgeford on 26 July 1917.

Airco DH.9A, No.B7664.

Sopwith F1 Camel No.H7000 of 209 Squadron. Despite its tatty appearance this is in fact a rebuilt aircraft after it was involved in a crash.

Captain R.H. Foss standing beside his Sopwith 1F Camel 'J' in Italy.

Sopwith 1½Strutter, A8286 built by Rushton and Proctor.

Sergeant Ted Ditchburn, RFC, tending to the engine of his Nieuport A6781 of No.40 Squadron, RFC, at Treizennes airfield, near Aire.

SPAD S VII Scout in RFC use.

Winners of an RFC sports day at Rang du Fliers receiving war bonds as prizes.

The Lord Mayor's Show, London, in 1917. An RFC Leyland lorry with a captured Halberstadt
D Scout aircraft on its back outside Marconi House.

The cockpit of the SE.5A.

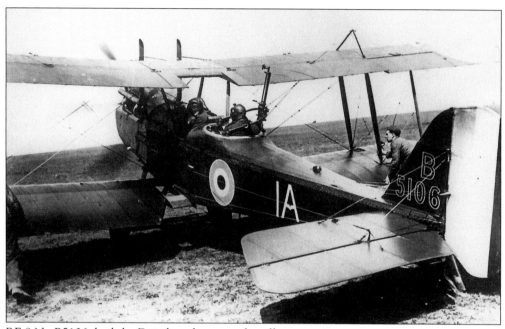

RE.8 No.B5106, built by Daimler, about to take off on a sortie.

Morane LA No.5120 of No.3 Squadron, RFC, being prepared for take-off.

Bristol M1C's of No.72 Squadron, RFC, in Mesopotamia, preparing for take-off.

Lt Arnold Shepherd in his Sopwith 1F1 Camel, about to take off on a sortie.

Captain E.L. Foot's Sopwith 1F1 Camel, No.B6398 'Cleopatra', of No.1 Squadron, RFC.

Refuelling a Sopwith 1F1 Camel by hand at No.204 TDS Eastchurch. The two officers were Canadian pupils.

Leyland transporter of the RFC at Helwan, Egypt, in 1917.

Sopwith F1 Camel No.F615 having its compass zeroed in by placing the aircraft on a revolving table and carrying out any adjustments necessary – Rang des Fleurs, 1917.

Sopwith F1 Camel, No.C42 'The White Feather' at Upavon. Even the twin Vickers machine guns were painted white.

Nieuport Triplane No.A6686 purchased from the French for testing by the RFC.

Captain Wendell Rogers of No.1 Squadron, RFC, at Bailleul on 27 December 1917 about to start the engine of his Nieuport 27, prior to going on patrol.

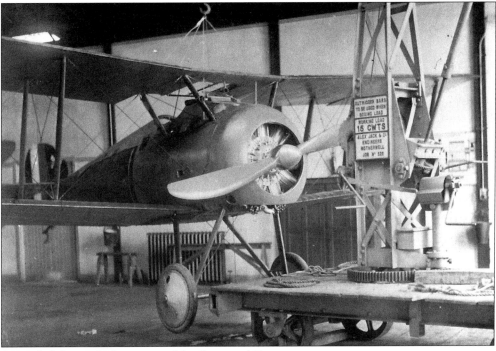

Sopwith Salamander being tested for Centre of Gravity.

SPAD S.VIIs at Hounslow preparing to take off.

Lieutenant Hobbs and Lieutenant Chippendale reporting their morning reconnaissance flight over the battlefield to Captain J.B. Solomon (Flight Commander) during the First Battle of Bapaume on 25 March 1918.

RE.8s being prepared for a patrol.

SE.5As of No.29 Squadron at Oudezeele about to go on patrol.

SE.5As of No.40
Squadron being
prepared for take-off.

Ground crews
attempting to remove
the wreckage of
possibly an RE.8 from
the top of a house and
shop after the engine
failed.

A mechanic assists the pilot and observer of an FE.2b of No.149 Squadron, RFC, to get dressed ready for a patrol. Note the photo flare hanging beneath the starboard wing of the FE.2b behind.

King George V inspecting fighter pilots of No.4 Squadron, Australian Flying Corps. The King is talking to Lieutenant R. King and Captain A.H. Cobby. At the King's right elbow is Major W.A. McCloughrey (CO of Squadron). In the foreground on the right is General Birdwood. Parade officers from left to right: Lts. W.C. Trescowthick, R.G. Smallwood, L.Bayer, R.B. Bennett, D.C. Carter, T.R. Edols, M.H. Eddie, L.T.E. Taplin. Although not strictly RFC, they were attached to the Royal Flying Corps as part of the Commonwealth forces.

RE.8s and Nieuport 17s of No.113 Squadron, lined up on Sarona airfield, Jaffa, Palestine.

Bristol M.1C of No.72 Squadron, RFC, in Mesopotamia, January 1918. The zigzag markings on the fuselage are almost certainly an individual pilot's markings.

Sopwith Pup, B2248, just minutes after its starboard undercarriage had collapsed after landing.

Sopwith 1F1 Camel, No.C.67 of 80 Squadron, RFC, being recovered by a German ground crew after being brought down by Jasta 11 (Richthofen's Squadron).

Martinsyde G102 in a 'desperate' situation after crashing into a field latrine on landing.

Sopwith Pup, C242, in a diamond livery.

The remains of Sopwith Pup, B5371 of No.43 Squadron, after a landing accident. The aircraft was flown by Lieutenant Henry R. Clay Junr, an American attached to the RFC for flight training.

Sopwith 1F Camel, No.D8101 of No.66 Squadron, RFC, flown by Lieutenant Gerald Birks, undergoing a service inside a canvas hangar.

Sopwith 1F Camel, No.B2455, 'X' of No.26 Squadron, RFC, flown by Lieutenant E.G. Forder, seen here at Feltre aerodrome after being shot down by Oberleutnant Linke Crawford of the Austro-Hungarian Air Service.

Lieutenant Jarvis about to get into the cockpit of his Sopwith 1F Camel, No.B6285, of No.28, Squadron, RFC.

Bristol F2b fighter, No.C4841, after an exceptionally heavy landing which, as can be seen, broke the back of the aircraft.

Wounded RFC officers recovering at the RFC Officers' Hospital in Eaton Square, London, in 1917.

DH.9 high in the clouds over the front relishing the tranquillity of flight, albeit for just a short time.

DH.6 trainer being refuelled for take-off at Netheravon.

Ground crew working on the engine of an RE.8 belonging to No.3 Squadron AFC at Premont.

Pronti a volare sulle linee tedesche
Un pilota britannico e il suo osservatore col loro "porta fortuna"

Italian postcards depicting British pilots. The caption reads 'Ready to fly over the German lines. A British pilot and his observer with their good luck charm', a pet dog.

Un originale
sostegno britannico
per telescopio,
fatto colla ruota
d'una bicicletta

Another Italian First World War postcard showing an RFC pilot looking through a telescope fixed to a bicycle wheel and front forks allowing it to be rotated as the aircraft moves.

Synchronization gear for the forward firing gun on an FE.2b.

Bristol F2b No.C4630 'J' of No.62 Squadron, RFC, after being shot down by Lieutenant Carl Delling of Jasta 3b.

Bristol F2b, No.A7107 '6' of No.48 Squadron, RFC, at Biggin Hill in August 191, seen here about to take off.

Captain
F.R. McCall of
No.16 Squadron,
RFC, examining a
photo-
reconnaissance
photograph. The
insignia on his
shoulder has been
scratched out by the
censor at the time.

Bristol F2b, No.A7231, of A Flight, No.11 Squadron, RFC, after being shot down relatively undamaged by Vzfw. Bey of Jasta 5. The crew, Lieutenants Scholz and Wookey were captured and made Prisoners of War. Wookey was threatened with a German Court Martial for carrying propaganda leaflets.

Bristol F2b, No.A7231 of No.11 Squadron, RFC, having been repaired and repainted by the Germans. The words 'Nicht Schiessen – Gute Leute' mean 'Don't Shoot – Good Luck'.

The original officers on No.40 Squadron, RFC, at Gosport. In the centre is the commanding officer, Major Robert Loraine.

The full complement of an RFC squadron thought to be No.22.

Officers of No.29 Squadron, RFC. From left to right: Lt W.L. Dougan, unknown USAS pilot, Lt Skiffer, Lt Singer.

Six nations are represented in this group: from left to right, sitting: Belgium, France, USAS; standing: South Africa, Britain, Australia. The RFC pilot standing in the centre was Japanese-born Flight Sergeant Ohara. He was awarded the Military Medal and was wounded six times.

Bristol Fighter of No.11 Squadron, RFC.

Training diagram of the RFC in 1917, 'Beware the Hun in the Sun'. In the foreground is a Bristol fighter, in the sun a Fokker Triplane and an Albatros D.III is coming in to attack.

No.85 Squadron at St. Omer lined up ready for a full squadron patrol. The nearest aircraft, C1904, was piloted by Captain K.K. Horn, MC, but was often used by Major W.A. 'Billy' Bishop, VC, DSO, MC, DFC. The second aircraft, D6851, was piloted by Lieutenant Elliot White Springs, an American, while the next in the line was piloted by the New Zealand 'Ace' Lieutenant C.R. McGregor. The CO at the time was Major Edward 'Micky' Mannock, VC, DSO, MC.

RFC/RAF air mechanics from No.22 Squadron armoury, Vert Galant airfield, checking the .303 ammunition belts for mal-positioning. This photograph was taken on 1 April 1918, the day the RFC became the RAF.

WRFC motor cyclist taking time out for a 'cuppa'. Note that the insignia on her uniform shows that of the Royal Flying Corps, but the motor cycle has RAF on the tank. This posed photograph was probably taken during the period when the change was just taking place.

Captain Horn, MC, of No.85 Squadron, RFC, about to slide into the cockpit of his Sopwith Dolphin.

Crews of A & B flights of No.22 Squadron, RFC, at Vert Galant aerodrome on 1 April 1918. From left to right: W.S. Hill (Canada), G.H. Traunweiser (Canada), J.H. Wallage, B.C. Budd, G.S. Hayward, S.J. Hunter, R. Critchley, W.F.J. Harvey, J.L. Morgan, H.F.Moore, H.B. Davison (Canada), J.E. Gurdon, Major J.A. McKelvie (CO), N.T. Barrington, Captain R.S. Boby, F.H. Harrison, Captain D.M. McGown. These crews had just returned from ground-strafing sorties against the retreating German army at the Somme.

Sopwith 1F Camel, 'J', of No.45 Squadron, RFC, in Italy about to go on patrol with Captain R.H. Foss in the cockpit.

Royal Aircraft Factory FE.2b of 149 Squadron at St. Omer. The pilot is seen examining one of the bombs that the armourer is about to place in the bomb rack beneath the wing of his aircraft.

SPADs of No.23 Squadron, RFC, lined up for inspection.

Major A.D. Carter, DSO, MC, seated in his SE.5A. Just to the left can be seen the Fokker D.VII in which Carter was later killed while testing the aircraft.

Allied Prisoners of War at the PoW camp at Karlsruhe with the camp's commanding officer while awaiting repatriation at the end of the war. Near the front, in hat and wearing a white kerchief, is the author Captain W.E. Johns, who wrote the very successful Biggles books.

Four

Metamorphosis:
From Air Corps
to Air Force.

Brigadier General Trenchard had been given the task of creating a new aerial force out of the meagre element of the RFC left behind in England in 1914: 116 aircraft (officially described as mainly junk), forty-one officers and several hundred airmen. With these limited resources he succeeded to some degree before he was posted to France to command No.1 Wing, RFC. In August 1915 Trenchard was promoted to command the entire RFC on active service.

Both the RFC and the RNAS had grown in strength to such an extent that they became unwieldy to manage as a global fighting force. In 1917, recognizing this situation, Lloyd George appointed a special committee – The Committee on Air Organization and Home Defence against Air Raids – chaired by the South African General Smuts, to enquire into and make recommendations as to the future of the two air services.

In mid-August 1917 the Smuts Committee made their report. It recommended that the RFC and the RNAS be amalgamated into a single air service and that an Air Ministry be established to control the new service.

On 29 November 1917 King George V gave Royal Assent to The Air Force Bill and, on 2 January 1918, the Air Ministry came into being. Major General Sir Hugh Trenchard, KCB, DSO, was appointed Chief of the Air Staff. Later he rose to the rank of Marshal of the Royal Air Force The Viscount Trenchard.

On 1 April 1918 the Royal Air Force – together with the Women's Royal Air Force – was formed by the amalgamation of the RFC and the RNAS. (Women had been employed in the RFC from early in 1917.)

The new Royal Air Force was the first independent Air Force in the world and – twenty-two years later – the most famous when it defeated the German Luftwaffe in the Battle of Britain.

Demobilisation! Although this cartoon is RAF not RFC, it can still be considered appropriate.